GIFT ITEM

This wonderful book was bought and generously given as a gift to

to : ______________________________

by: ______________________________

on the occasion of

____

dated

____

If you received this book as a gift, it means that you are special and the giver thinks real well of you. Congratulations.

May God bless you and give you wisdom as you study this book.

TRAIN ME

TRAIN ME

The yearning of every child

ABINYE D. C. NWANKWO

TRAIN ME – The yearning of every child

Scripture quotations marked (KJV) are taken from the King James Version of the Holy Bible.

Scripture quotations marked (NIV) are taken from the New International Version of the Holy Bible.

Scripture quotations marked (CEV) are taken from the Contemporary English Version of the Holy Bible.

Scripture quotations marked (ASV) are taken from the American Standard Version of the Holy Bible.

Scripture quotations marked (GNB) are taken from the Good News Bible.

Scripture quotations marked (AMP) are taken from the Amplified Bible.

SECOND EDITION

First published in Nigeria by
COMMANDING WEALTH
commandingwealth.ng@gmail.com
+2348033805280

ISBN: 979-8-3541-9323-3

Free edition was first published & printed in 2010
Second edition was first published & printed in 2013

DEDICATED TO

The E-series
(My wonderful children)

CONTENT

FOREWORD xi
ACKNOWLEDGEMENT xv
PREFACE xvii
INTRODUCTION xix

CHAPTER ONE (**LITTLE FOXES**) 1
Lack of Time with Family 3
Lack of Love 6
Lack of Discipline 7
Lack of Provision...9

CHAPTER TWO (**THE PLACE OF THE CANE**)........................... 13
Beat Or Speak 15
When they are young enough 17

CHAPTER THREE (**HOUSE-HELPS**)... 25

CHAPTER FOUR (**DRESSING**) 33

CHAPTER FIVE (**FINANCE**) 37
Budgeting Skills 41
Allowance To Children...42
Financial Slave Trade 45

CHAPTER SIX (**SEX EDUCATION**) 49

CHAPTER SEVEN (**THE CAMERA**) 55
Spotted And Speckled 57
Watch The Gates 60
The Prayer Of The Three Fishes 63

CHAPTER EIGHT (**ADVISE TO PARENTS**) 69

FEEDBACK PAGE

REFERENCES

ABOUT THE AUTHOR

FOREWORD

When Samson's imminent birth was prophesied by the angel, his parents did something I think every parent should do – they went to God to ask him how to train the child for him to fulfil his prophetic destiny (Judges 13).

Bro. Abinye Nwankwo in this book, ***Train Me***, has provided both parents and prospective parents with clear Scriptural counsel that, if applied, will enable their children to fulfil divine purpose.

The title of the book is a rebuke of sorts and an indictment of parents—the child, to get our wavering attention, cries out, "**Train Me**!" as if we had been too busy with other things and negligent in the very important assignment of properly training the next generation! And if truth be told, many of us parents have been negligent. We are not giving our children sufficient attention because we are too busy with so many other things.

The book contains practical and helpful insights. For instance, Bro. Abinye says, even if the child did not quite succeed at what he had set out to accomplish, the parent should praise the effort the child had put in! Then he adds, "I encourage you to start looking for more opportunities to catch them doing good so you can praise them. Don't be a 'fault-finder,' be a 'good-finder.'" Among many insightful thoughts on money matters that you will find in the book is the advice to introduce our children with care to the automatic teller machine (ATM) facility so that the child does not grow up to disdain hard work but rather begins to think that all you need to do is to slot a piece of plastic in some machine and presto, money will come tumbling into your laps! Many other crucial subjects are discussed, such as how and when to bring up the recurrent, vexing issue of sex with your child and the place of the ubiquitous househelps and what to do with them.

Bro. Abinye has written from divine inspiration, from his many years of experience as a committed teacher in the children's ministry and, very importantly, from the vantage and privileged position of a man who himself is a parent.

This book will be worth the money and time you invest in it. Therefore, read it meditatively and then put it into practise diligently!

Yehuwdah E. Chad-Umoren, Ph. D
President, Spirit of Revelation Ministry International
Port Harcourt

TRAIN ME

Poem written by Upadhizhi ThankGod

I can be good and bad
I can be wild and mild
Do not ignore me but adore me
Because I have been put in your womb
So why go for an abortion when you have a vision

Why put me to struggle
I just want to be cuddled
I am an arrow in God's hands sent to you
So I won't bring sorrow to you

I am the next generation
Feed me with the spiritual milk
That I may grow up to salvation

Even when I go offline
All I ask is that you bring me back online
Because God's line is the best network
For you to train a child like me.

ACKNOWLEDGEMENT

I am grateful to God Almighty for the inspiration given to me to put down this generational book.

I bless God for my parents Late Rev. Can. and Dr(Mrs) I. A. Nwankwo for training me and for the discipline they instilled in me. My mother did a great work in correcting technical errors in this book.

Thanks be to God for the wonderful parents of my graceful wife, Rev. Can. and Mrs. C. M. Sorgwe, without them I would not have had this peaceful well-trained woman as wife.

I say thank you to my early mentors and parents in the Lord – Elder S. N. Solomon and Pastor Oribi Nathan.

I am also grateful to God for some clergy men who had challenged and encouraged me while I served as coordinator of the Children Ministry in the Chapel of the Transfiguration – Late Ven.(Prof)

T.N. Okujagu, Ven. Dr. Ben Onu, Rev. Chris Sunday and Rev. Amos Osaromkpe.

I express sincere gratitude to one of my daughters in the Lord, Miss Upadhizhi ThankGod, who at short notice wrote a poem –Train Me – to go along with this book. I also pray God's blessings on all those who as children and teenagers have listened to teachings while I served in the Children Ministry.

Pastor (Dr) Y. E. Chad-Umoren despite his busy schedule accepted to read through and write the foreword to this book. He is one of my mentors and I truly appreciate him.

Thanks to my darling wife, Mrs. Mercy Nwankwo for being a virtuous wife, raising godly children and for correcting some typographical errors in this book.

And to you reading this book, I am grateful. Pass on the message; we need well-disciplined children to have a better future. I love you.

Engr. Abinye D.C. Nwankwo

PREFACE

The first thing a child does when entering this world at birth is to cry (Many folks have attached reasons to it), but I have come to understand that as that baby grows, there is a yearning in his heart - *train me*. The children are indeed yearning to be trained. Contrary to the cry of their heart, some have been abandoned and dumped by selfish parents, while others have been cared for but not properly trained. This book comes in handy for those who sincerely want the best for their children and society at large.

The initial edition of the book, TRAIN ME, which was printed in 2010 and distributed free, was written within one week as God gave inspiration. Since then, there has been a desire to study more, get criticism and contributions from other people. Therefore, I now present a fuller edition.

The book exposes some of the *foxes* that seek to destroy the family. It also opens up the concept of *the use of the cane for* discipline. The issue of

Househelps - is it good or bad? - is also tactically handled in chapter three.

Dressing, finance, and sex education are three areas, amongst others, in which children are yearning for direction. These are handled in chapters four, five, and six, respectively. This is a book to study and keep as a reference. There is no particular order in which to study the chapters.

This book has been commended for its thought-provoking nature. It is recommended as a valuable gift to all newlyweds, prospective mothers and fathers, teachers in schools, and as a creditable working tool for the clergy and counsellors. It is a wonderful gift that you can give to any family or friend.

At the end of each chapter, there are exercises that will help you test your level of understanding of the chapter. Do not bypass any questions. Do not stop halfway; you will come forth as gold. It is like a manual, which you may need to consult time after time.

INTRODUCTION

TRAIN ME (The yearning of every child)! The word "train" is synonymous with the word "coach". One characteristic of a coach is that he puts in his best effort knowing what is ahead. Similarly, training a child requires that parents put in their best(which could mean working hard to take care of the children). Also, a good coach does not give up, and even when he feels discouraged, he does not show it in front of his trainees. Similarly, a good parent would not give up on his child. But note, the earlier you start giving your child/wards proper training, the easier it will be to live in good health. It is easier to train a child than to repair an adult. Preventive maintenance is far cheaper than corrective maintenance.

It is indeed worthy to note that family life does not follow a regular algorithm in that, in many institutions, certificates are awarded to a person when he/she graduates. But in marriage - the marriage certificate comes at the beginning of the course (that could mean nobody believes in the failure of a marriage or that there is no graduation). Also, as Harold Sala noted, "To drive a car,... or practise medicine, you must be licensed—indicating that you have a certain level of training and expertise in performing that function'," but with parenting and training a child, no licence is required. Someone may ask, "Where is the manual that comes with a new baby?" Yet it rests on you to study to 'show yourself approved'. I will interchangeably use the words "book" and "manual" for what you are reading now. And the word "children" could be used to include teenagers.

Are you a parent or a children's teacher, be it in school or in church? This manual is for you. Prayerfully study it. I pray that the eyes of your understanding will be enlightened. Read through to the end. Even if some points may look old-fashioned, they are based on an Old Book – The BIBLE. Whether you are a Christian or not, this book is for you. The decadence in our society affects all. If only we could properly direct children, our society might have a brighter future

CHAPTER ONE

LITTLE FOXES

Songs of Solomon 2:15 *"Take us the foxes, the little foxes, that spoil the vines, for our vines have tender grapes (KJV)*

What are foxes? The Encarta dictionary elaborately defines a fox as "a carnivorous animal of the dog family that has a pointed muzzle, large ears, a long bushy tail, and usually reddish brown or gray fur." It went on to say that "Foxes are found throughout most of the world and hunt alone, mainly at night, relying on cunning and an acute sense of hearing and smell."

Foxes are known to be cunning and crafty. Hence, as we study this chapter, we will note some little foxes which could appear simple yet are very dangerous to the vine.

The **vine** represents the family, and from our first scripture above, each vine has fruit, in this case – **tender grapes**. These represent the children in the home. As is appropriately portrayed in the book of psalms;

> ***Psalm 127:3*** *"Lo, children are an heritage of the Lord; and the fruit of the womb is his reward."(KJV)*

Hence, children are the fruits of the home. Back to the initial scripture; there are little foxes militating against the vineyard(the family) and targeting the tender grapes(the children). The Bible instructs us to catch those foxes before they catch us.

These foxes are crafty and do *things* that we, as parents or guardians, usually take for granted. Let's identify some foxes that target children(the tender grapes);

Lack of Time with Family

Some people are too busy or selfish to have quality time with their family members. Parents ought to make time to train their children. Let us consider the instance of a coach. Which team would most probably do better—a team whose coach spent only two weeks in training or a team whose coach spent six months? If you answer that question without bias, you will admit that quality time spent with one's children cannot be overemphasized.

Quality time spent with one's children cannot be overemphasized

Proverbs 22:6 *Train up a child in the way he should go; and when he is old, he shall not depart from it. (KJV)*

Proverbs 22:6 *Point your kids in the right direction- when they're old they won't be lost. (Message Version)*

Get it right; it is easier to train a child than to repair an adult. Because the days are evil, you will have to pay for every time you mismanage (Ephesians 5:16). Many parents believe that spending the majority of their time with their children is exhausting, so they have delegated the sole responsibility of training them to third parties known as house-helps. If you get tired of handling little children, what would you do when they get older and probably get out of hand? Put in mind what the scripture says;

> ***Jeremiah 12:5*** *...' If you have raced with men on foot and they have tired you out, then how can you compete with horses?...' (AMP)*

I would like to add a contribution made by someone who came across the initial edition of this book, *TRAIN ME.*

> *In as much as parents work from 9am to 5pm to keep the family wheel moving, they SHOULD NOT substitute the peace of the family for a meager sum they receive at the end of the month. Parents should know that these children are*

God's and were only entrusted to them for care. Parents should love their children by all means {provide for them}, for they brought them into this world. Parents should as a matter of fact help build up their {child/ward's} self esteem {self confidence}::::by being a source of encouragement to them in times when they feel downcast or defeated....Parents can BOND more by eating, strolling, chatting, playing, helping with assignments and school work etc. Parents should protect their child/ward from all forms of danger or anything that poses a threat. [some parents really DO NOT CARE]. - Chipuruime Mbonu

I quite agree that with the so called 'busy schedule', some parents no more eat at the same time or even have time to stroll with their children. It is often said, 'no talking while eating', yet eating together with your children/wards helps you to feel their pulse and mood.

Lack of Love

The law of osmosis states that a solvent flows by diffusion through a semi-permeable membrane from a less concentrated solution to a more concentrated one.

Similarly, the teenager or child tends to flow to where they will seemingly find more love. This little fox has caused great problems like teenage pregnancy, rape, cult initiation, etc. I learnt that if a mother duck does not teach the ducklings in the first two days to follow her, the ducklings will learn to follow and have emotional attachment to any moving object, like a block of wood floating on water. Similarly, attract your kids with love. Please love them and show it. Not just your children, but everyone under your care and tutelage. (*To the children who may come across this book: no matter what happens at home, it is not right to destroy your integrity and testimony outside. Remember that the devil would even pretend to show love in order to destroy you. For he (the devil) has the ministry of stealing, killing, and destroying* - John 10:10)

Lack of Discipline

According to Proverbs 23:13,14;

> *"Don't be afraid to correct your young ones; a spanking won't kill them. A good spanking, in fact, might save them from something worse than death". (Message Version)*

There should be a place for discipline at home. It is not enough to say ‘we are praying for them’, because if you only pray for them (and not correct them) when they do wrong, they could continue in the act in order to make you a *prayer warrior*. The Bible says, "beat them’ (in an age-appropriate manner), and they shall not die, rather ‘you'll save their souls from hell’.

One man facing the firing squad was asked for his last wish, which was to privately tell his mother something in her ears. As she came close, he bit her ears with his teeth, saying she never corrected him as a child when he displayed those characteristics. Parents, when that little girl in your house starts moving with strange men, do not just sit back and say, 'my daughter is growing up', *point them to Christ.*

Proverbs 22:6(message version) says;

> *"Point your kids in the right direction- when they're old they won't be lost".*

No form of discipline appears to be pleasant, but the outcome could be beautiful. Hebrews 12:11(TLB) informs us that;

> *"Being punished isn't enjoyable while it is happening-it hurts! But afterwards we can see the result, a quiet growth in grace and character".*

And according to Psalms 119:67(GNT);

> *"Before you punished me, I used to go wrong, but now I obey your word".*

While Psalms 119:71(GNT) says that

> *"My punishment was good for me, because it made me learn your commands".*

Today, I can look back and rejoice because my parents disciplined me. Would your kids be able to thank you for how you had moulded them positively via discipline?

Lack of Provision

> *"But if a man makes no provision for those dependent on him (children, wards...), and especially for his own family, he has disowned the faith and is behaving worse than an unbeliever".* ***1Timothy 5:8****(The Weymouth New Version)*

Are you there, always donating millions to social groups and even churches, yet you do not provide for the basic needs of your children and those depending on you (including the ones you call house-helps)? The Bible says you are not just an unbeliever but worse. We are talking about the little foxes that break into the family. Are you committed as a man to sending recharge cards to ladies outside while your wife and children are begging to be attended to? The Bible says you are worse than an infidel.

Hey, we have seen some of the little foxes, what's next? "*Catch the foxes for us, the little foxes that ruin vineyards. Our vineyards are blooming.*" Songs of Solomon 2:15(God's Word version).

CATCH them (Lack of time with family, Lack of love, Lack of discipline, and Lack of provision), and lay them at the foot of the cross of Jesus, and have them destroyed. Build your home and bring your children/teenagers to GOD.

EXERCISES

1. Quote Songs of Solomon 2:15

2. Why is it difficult in some homes to see parents and their children eating together on the dining table? It is still seen on movies anyway. What obtains in your home?

3. When last did you get a gift (no matter how small) for your child to demonstrate your love?

4. Do you discipline your children and wards when they do wrong? And can you boldly say you do so with a heart of love?

CHAPTER TWO

THE PLACE OF THE CANE

Some people say 'I do not need cane in my house, I love my child'. Hear what the Holy Book says in

> ***Proverbs 13:24*** *He that spareth his rod hateth his son: but he that loveth him chasteneth him betimes. (KJV)*

If you do not flog your child when he knowingly does wrong, it is a sign that you hate that child. The word 'rod' (rod of discipline/correction) refers to a cane, not a metal rod or a plumbing pipe. **Proverbs 22:15**(AMP) has this to say that

> *"Foolishness is bound up in the heart of a child, but the rod of discipline will drive it far from him".*

I like the way the Good News Bible Translation puts the first part of Proverbs 22:15 in plain words;

> *"Children just naturally do silly, careless things"*

but the rod of discipline is the tool necessary to drive foolishness far from the child.

Now let us partake in a brief exposition of some passages of Scripture.

> ***Numbers 20:8*** *Take the rod, and gather thou the assembly together, thou, and Aaron thy brother, and speak ye unto the rock before their eyes; and it shall give forth his water, and thou shalt bring forth to them water out of the rock: so thou shalt give the congregation and their beasts drink. (KJV)*

> ***Numbers 20:11*** *And Moses lifted up his hand, and with his rod he smote the rock twice: and the water came out abundantly, and the congregation drank, and their beasts also. (KJV)*

> ***Proverbs 23:13*** *Withhold not correction from the child: for if thou beatest him with the rod, he shall not die. Thou shalt beat him with the rod, and shalt deliver his soul from hell. (KJV)*

Beat Or Speak

Some may wonder what the above passages (the first two) have to do with the disciplining of children. Let us explore the scripture a little. God gave Moses an instruction to **speak** to the rock, and instead Moses **beat** the rock. Anyway it still brought forth water but Moses suffered for it.

In terms of discipline, God says **beat** the child, but instead some parents only **speak** in anger to the child. Just like in the case of Moses, the child may be corrected at the moment, but you may suffer for it. There are children who are living under a curse that their parents spoke into their lives in anger, and the parents are seeking in tears for God to deliver their adult-children from stupidity.

Some have spoken coconut head into their children and wards.

If you use the wrong tool for a particular job, you may get the job done but you would likely injure yourself. Use the cane to drive foolishness away from that ***young*** child. And scripture urges you to do it in love. Do not injure the child, yet flog the child in such a way that he/she feels the pain. Few minutes after I beat my daughter hard with the cane, I embraced her. She cried awhile and stayed with me. Gradually I see the foolishness running away.

If you use the wrong tool for a particular job, you may get the job done but you would likely injure yourself

Point to note; you should endeavour to be sure the child knows why he/she is flogged. And many times be sure that the wrong was intentional. May the Lord grant you wisdom.

Let us look at the next passage in two translations;

Proverbs 19:18 *Chasten thy son while there is hope, and let not thy soul spare for his crying. (KJV)*

Proverbs 19:18 *Discipline your children while they are young enough to learn. If you don't, you are helping them destroy themselves. (GNB)*

When they are young enough

While there is still hope, discipline with the cane. The passage portrays a scenario where there will come a time when there will be no more hope in terms of beating with the cane. The second version makes it clearer. Discipline when the child is still young enough. I have seen parents beat BIG children with the cane, it had little or no impact. Hence, at a particular stage, what the grown-up child may need more is counselling.

Some may ask; at what age would you consider a child young? That question could be knotty. WHY? Each child is unique, some crawl at five months, and some at eight months. Some are weaned at a year old, some at two years. What am I saying? Start early to discipline your child. Do not wait till there is no hope.

Being disciplined cannot guarantee that your child will be automatically disciplined

Hello Parents, discipline is not genetic. Being disciplined cannot guarantee that your child will be automatically disciplined.

Some people even believe that being anointed by God automatically entitles them to well-trained children, but that is a false assumption taken too far. Consider the biblical figure of Eli the priest:

> ***1Samuel 2:12*** *The sons of Eli were base and worthless; they did not know or regard the Lord. (AMP)*

> ***1Samuel 3:13*** *For I have told him that I will judge his house for ever for the iniquity which he knoweth; because his sons made themselves vile, and he restrained them not. (KJV)*

Eli was anointed yet his sons were worthless because he did not restrain them (lack of discipline). It appears to me that Eli did only *speaking* with no *beating*;

> ***1Samuel 2:22a, 23, 24***
>
> *Eli was now very old. He kept hearing about everything his sons were doing to the Israelites ...*
>
> *So he said to them, "Why are you doing these things? Everybody tells me about the evil you are doing. Stop it, my sons! This is an awful thing the people of the LORD are talking about! (GNT)*

With all his talking, God still said in 1 Samuel 3:13 that Eli did not restrain his sons. These children led to their father's death.

Samuel, another anointed man, would have made a similar mistake concerning training his children properly; despite the fact that he witnessed what happened to Eli's family.

> ***1Samuel 8:1-3*** *And it came to pass, when Samuel was old, that he made his sons judges over Israel. Now the name of his firstborn was Joel; and the name of his second, Abiah: they were judges in Beersheba. And his sons walked not in his ways, but turned aside after lucre, and took bribes, and perverted judgment. (KJV)*

Preachers or holy men should handle the issue of proper discipline seriously with trembling. Eli and Samuel did not get it right. The Bible says 'work out your salvation with fear and trembling' (slightly out of context though). You can get it right if the right principles are applied. Use the cane when necessary **and let not thy soul spare for his crying**(Prov. 19:18)

Please do not beat beyond the offence commited. Some parents/guardians store up offences; they say to the child, *'you did this two weeks ago, and did that a week ago, and did these today – I will show you today'* Hence they flog the child/ward based on two weeks' offence – That is wrong. Harold Sala wrote, "love without discipline is not love, and discipline apart from love is only punishment". I heard the story of Sean Paddock, a four-year-old boy who died after his mother wrapped him so tightly in blankets for making a mistake and he was unable to breathe. That is not discipline; it is murder. On the other hand, some parents do not want their children to be touched with a cane. Several years ago in the Children's Ministry, I met a man who was offended because his daughter was disciplined in church. "Why did you discipline my child with a cane?" he demanded angrily of the children's teacher. "The Bible says - the rod of correction," the teacher replied. The man (who was well-respected in society) decided to prevent

> **Love without discipline is not love, and discipline apart from love is only punishment**
>
> *-Harold Sala-*

his daughter from attending church. I'm not sure if he thought the "rod of correction" would cause him to lose his child. He actually lost his daughter to illness before she entered an institution of higher learning. Many have threatened to remove their children from church if they feel insulted. There are parents today whose children attend very good schools, but because a teacher 'insulted' them by correcting their child, they stopped the child from going to school - VERY PATHETIC!

EXERCISES

1. Which best describes the 'rod of correction'?
   (a) Metallic chain used to bind criminals
   (b) Plumbing rod
   (c) Simple cane used to instil discipline in a child
   (d) Figurative statement for pots and solid objects used on the heads of stubborn children

2. As a parent, have you ever cursed your children or wards staying in your house?

3. If God should answer every word you use on your children; what would your fate be? (Read Numbers 14:27-29)

CHAPTER THREE

HOUSE-HELPS

Many people seeing this topic will quickly rush to it. But be prepared because what you are expecting to hear may not be what is written in this manual. I have seen people who would rather be on their own than get house-helps because of what they heard about them.

There are people, even Christians, who believe nothing good can come out of a person who is a **houseboy** or **housegirl**, as they are popularly called. Some feel house-helps are usually witches or 'mammy-water'. I do not hold it against them, for I have heard of a housegirl who used a pestle to pound the leg of the baby she was meant to care for.

Many fear and believe that house-helps are husband and wife snatchers, and unfortunately it came upon them according to their faith. It is written in Job 3:25(ASV), " For the thing which I fear cometh upon me, And that which I am afraid of cometh unto me. "

NOTE: when I use the term house-helps, the scope of this manual covers only those who are either children or teenagers.

If you can stay without a house-help, please do. But if you desire to have one, make up your mind to take good care of them, treat them like children of a human being and most importantly, of God. Consider it old fashion to feed house-helps with dog's plate. Buy good clothes for them as you buy for your children. If you care for them properly, they would be able to translate the care to your children. A friend of mine came for a weekend in my apartment, when he left the next day, he

If you can stay without a house-help, please do. But if you desire to have one, make up your mind to take good care of them

commented that the house-helps were always happy. He said he felt they were my direct siblings.

There were several house-helps recorded in the scripture, an example of which was Joseph in Egypt. Many bad names given to house-helps are sometimes insinuated by the so-called leaders in the house. Let us consider Joseph's situation.

> ***Genesis 39:17,18*** *Then she said, "That Hebrew slave of yours tried to rape me!*

But when I screamed for help, he left his coat and ran out of the house." (CEV)

Joseph was a house-help, and he was termed a wife snatcher or rapist for what he did not even do. There are many house-helps who have been so accused falsely. These are children who could make it in life.

Sarah made her servant girl to sleep with her husband. Some women today are in Sarah's stead, making their husbands to do the unthinkable: Think of a married woman who always wears clothes that are out of shape and smelly, while the girls staying with them always wear sporty and attractive clothes. Imagine a woman who would always nag and torment her husband, while others appreciate him.

> ***Proverbs 21:9*** *Better to live on the roof than share the house with a nagging wife. (Today's English Version)*

It is wrong for a woman to keep her husband on the roof and let another girl to bring him down from the roof. However, that is no reason for a man to go into immorality. But thou art inexcusable, O man (Romans 12:1). There is nothing that should justify a man going into immorality.

There is nothing that should justify a man going into immorality

Please do not lead your house-helps to do evil – If you are a Christian, lead them to Christ. Even in scripture, there are godly house-helps. Joseph was one of such. We also have the case of Naaman's slave girl in 2 Kings 5:1-4. It is so sweet to have everyone in your household serving God.

> ***Acts 10:2*** *Cornelius was a very religious man. He worshiped God, and so did everyone else who lived in his house. He had given a lot of money to the poor and was always praying to God. (CEV)*

Cornelius was a happy man because everyone (that includes house-helps/servants) in his house worshiped God with him.

> ***Acts 16:31-33*** *They replied, "Have faith in the Lord Jesus and you will be saved! This is also true for everyone who lives in your home."*
>
> *Then Paul and Silas told him and everyone else in his house about the Lord.*
>
> *While it was still night, the jailer took them to a place where he could wash their cuts and bruises. Then he and everyone in his home were baptized. (CEV)*

If you believe that your biological children can be godly, **This is also true for everyone who lives in your home** (including house-helps). Permit me to put it this way – 'this is also true for your house-helps'. If you believe that your children can be saved, 'this is also true for your house-helps'. If you believe your children should eat good food, 'this is also true for your house-helps'. If you believe your children could put on good clothes, 'this is also true for your house-helps'.

They would be better helps if they know Christ. If you study the book of Philemon in the Bible, Philemon had a 'useless' house-help(slave) called Onesimus. After Onesimus gave his life to Christ, he became more than a 'useful' brother.

Buy gifts and clothes for them, but my advice is – husbands and wives – care for them as a couple not individually. And do not give the devil any chance to destroy your home.

Proper disciplinary action also applies to house-helps. When necessary make use of normal cane on them, not pots or frying pan. Do not hit their heads on the wall or curse them in the name of your great grand ancestors. They are human beings like your children.

> ***1Timothy 5:8*** *"But if a man makes no provision for those dependent on him(children, wards...), and especially for his own family, he has disowned the faith and is behaving worse than an unbeliever". (The Weymouth New Version)*

As mention earlier; are you there, always donating millions to social groups and even churches, yet you do not provide for the basic needs of your children and those depending on you (including the ones you call house-helps). The Bible says you are not just an unbeliever but worse.

Please note:

This manual focuses on training and caring for the child/teenager. Hence some other things concerning house-helps may be found in marriage counselling books

It is also important to investigate who you are bringing to your home, their parents and background, but if you made up your mind to live with them, also make up your mind to take good care of them

EXERCISES

1. Which is most probable, when a house-help is properly cared for and well trained? They
   (a) do more harm.
   (b) translate the care to your children.
   (c) enter into witchcraft.

2. In what way does a wife cause her husband to go up the roof? By
   (a) constant nagging.
   (b) the perfume she puts on.
   (c) snoring when sleeping.

3. Is it a righteous thing to give your children good food, and then arrange the crumbs that fall from the children's table into food for a house-help? Yes/No

CHAPTER FOUR

DRESSING

Dressing has become an issue today, many have asked if God is interested in our outward appearance even as adults not to talk of a child. There are several things the scripture said concerning the issue which are beyond the scope of this book. But let us track what transpired in Genesis 3.

> ***Genesis 3:7*** *As soon as they had eaten it, they were given understanding and realized that they were naked; so they sewed fig leaves together and covered themselves. (GNB)*

> ***Genesis 3:21*** *For Adam also and for his wife the Lord God made long coats (tunics) of skins and clothed them. (AMP)*

Before what happened in Gen 3:7, man did not know good and evil, similar to a new born baby, but in verse 7 - it is recorded that *they had understanding*, they knew when to hide. When one of my daughters was two years old, if I cautioned her about putting a particular item in her mouth and she desired to do it, she would run to another room where I would not see her in order to put it back in her mouth. This indicates that she had started to know what was good and bad.

It may interest you to know that the first correction God gave to man after he understood(his eyes were open), was in his dressing. Adam and Eve sewed an indecent dress with fig leaves. It could have been transparent (since it was made of leaves) or too short. Hence God had to replace it for them. In verse 2, according to the Amplified version, God made a **long** garment for them. It was not a mini dress.

The point I am making here is that if God took time to teach man how to dress after he started to understand good and bad, then the best time to teach someone good dressing habits is as a child (as soon as they start to understand things). Many of the young folks in higher institutions indulging in indecent dressing are showing the dressing habits they were moulded with. It may be argued that some learn to use the left hand at old age, but if we help our children now, we could have a safer future in this nation and beyond. Remember, "Train up a child in the way he should go, and when he is old, he will not stray" (Proverbs 22:6).

The best time to teach someone good dressing habits is as a child

To add an important point, a dress, apart from being a covering, is also for *beauty*. Hence, sew beautiful, colourful clothes for your children. Every child deserves to be beautiful.

Train your children to dress properly. I believe that we are aware that there are dresses that appeal sexually, and such dresses place your children in a position to experience sexual victimization or to become promiscuous. Dear parents, be clear about your values. We need to show our kids that we value them for who they are.

EXERCISES

1. Has God ever shown interest in anyone's clothing? .... (Yes/No)

2. From your words and action, have you ever encouraged your child to appear sexy? ....

3. When is the best time to start teaching a child about dressing habits?

(a) At 15 years of age

(b) Immediately they are born

(c) When they start to understand good and evil

CHAPTER FIVE

FINANCE

For which of you, intending to build a tower, sitteth not down first, and counteth the cost, whether he have sufficient to finish it? Lest haply, after he hath laid the foundation, and is not able to finish it, all that behold it begin to mock him, Saying, This man began to build, and was not able to finish.

Luke 14:28-30 (KJV)

The man in the above passage had a poor financial inclination. He seemed not to have the proper budgeting skills. If children were not to grow to become adults, then teaching them finance might as well not be much of a concern. But we (adults) were once children, and the difficulty we now face with our financial habits is not detached from our upbringing. Hence, we must make every effort to raise financially well-disciplined children. Start exposing your children to good money habits so that they can understand the concept and value of money as they get older. If you teach your children an appropriate balance between spending and saving, you could save them from future disaster.

Avoiding financial difficulty is not about dishing out money uncontrollably when they ask for anything. Fred G. Gosman opines that "Children who always get what they want will want as long as they live.". Also, the statement by Taylor Cameron is an eye opener, "Do not give your kids money, give them *education* and *opportunity*. It costs a lot less and will develop the productive children you desire." I would add that if you must give them money, it should be for the purpose of giving them an *opportunity* to learn the concept and value of money. Therefore, teach them the relationship between *work* and *money*. As a children's teacher in church, I love the scripture in Proverbs 22:6 which admonishes parents to train their children properly. While it is not my intention to condemn anyone, how do you envision the future for a child sent to a school where someone is paid to dress his bed, wash his clothes, bring food to his dormitory, and so on? Quoting from the book *The Millionaire Mentality by Dexter Yager & Doug Wead* it says, "Children must be taught to develop work habits... they must be taught to work for their own money and therefore learn its value'.

In order to motivate your child to learn the virtue of saving money, you need to make the child to understand that money earned is tied to effort or work done. When children frequently observe you drawing out cash from the ATM, they could feel that all you need to do is - put in a card and money will gush out. They may not understand, unless properly educated, that it takes effort to make money. Hence, when they learn what is involved in making money, they will be spurred to save. Provide a safe place for the

Children who always get what they want will want as long as they live

-Fred G. Gosman-

younger kids to save their money, and as they grow older, educate them on the accumulation of interest. Then they can be introduced to the banking system. When I was much younger, I started saving money in a metal container with a replaceable lid and a small hole on the lid. Fortunately or unfortunately, I learnt a lesson; After saving for a while, I noticed that the container was so light, I opened it up to find out that all my savings were gone (it would not have just disappeared-it was *stolen*). I learnt that there is a risk in *almost everything,* including saving money. I later upgraded to opening a savings account in a bank as a teenager. Speaking about risk in savings, the scripture also mentions a situation where someone must have regretted saving money in an unskilful manner by digging a hole.

Matthew 25:18,26,27

18 But the man with the single thousand dug a hole and carefully buried his master's money. 26 "The master was furious. 'That's a terrible way to live! It's criminal to live cautiously like that! If you knew I was after the best, why did you do less than the least? 27 The least you could have done would have been to invest the sum with the bankers, where at least I would have gotten a little interest. (The Message Bible)

Budgeting Skills

The Encarta dictionary defines budget as a plan for allocating resources: "a plan specifying how resources, especially time or money, will be allocated or spent during a particular period". This would mean that for a child to be taught budgeting skills, he/she should have the resource(time or money) to practice with. (More would be said on resources in the section on Allowances).

Teaching your children on the subject of budget may require some prerequisite *courses (as it were)* in **Prioritizing**, and **Making best bargains**. Hence, at an early but appropriate age, take your children along with you when you go to stores or supermarkets. Let them locate and read out the unit prices of different items and make the best bargains. As they grow into teens, let them participate in some areas of the family budget and in making market lists. Teach them how to create budgets that include both short- and long-term goals (including savings).

They could sometimes bring a list of items they need, decide not to purchase all of them, and make it an *opportunity* for them to learn how to prioritize. Sticking to one's budget could mean sacrificing and giving up some things. Parents should not use this paragraph as an excuse to be stingy with their children. Teach them to differentiate "wants" from "needs. Some parents unconsciously teach their kids to purchase unnecessary things on impulse.

Allowance To Children

SHOULD I GIVE ALLOWANCES TO MY CHILDREN? This is a very good topic for debate. it has indeed led to arguments amongst parents. Some say *why not?* Others say *if you give an allowance for chores, then they would always ask for pay for everything.* Two sets of people in their statement *seem* to be on different sides;

Taylor Cameron says, "Do not give your kids money, give them education and opportunity"

Dexter Yager & Doug Wead it say, "they must be taught to work for their own money and therefore learn its value'.

But we need to give the children an *opportunity* to learn. In the definition of budget, there was the word "resources," which are needed as a tool in budgeting. You should not give them mere lectures without practicals to simulate what they are taught. There is what is known as "simulation" in industries for learning or training purposes. A "simulation" environment is usually safe. For instance, to study the effect of an impact on a car falling down a cliff, it could be simulated in a computer software environment, so there is no physical damage. Also, giving your child an opportunity to earn some cash to practise budgeting, savings, and other financial skills is a good way for them to manage cash in a safe environment. If they make a bad financial decision, it is not fatal as the amount involved is small (though to them it may appear large). Some parents have allowed their children to grow into adulthood and allowed them to go into marriage and jobs without any good *simulation*. Hence, some people have made errors in investments that cost them their lives.

In order to provide the opportunity to learn, provide a little allowance when they do some chores beyond their normal everyday duties. You could let them *wash the car, weed the grass, or do some extra work* to make a small amount of money. From the age of six or seven, a child should be able to handle some tasks that require an allowance.

One parent says that chores and the associated pay rate are written on a board for their children. Hence, their children mark chores done and calculate their expected pay. The parent also noted that as the children grow older, some of those chores are to be done without pay, and others are added at probably higher rates. That is the formula the parent used. Each parent could have his/her own formula to give the children an opportunity to learn to handle money.

Financial Slave Trade

Consider the fiction below:

Mrs. Brown called her eight-year-old son one Tuesday morning. "Kolade, go and borrow some maggi cubes from madam Okon, then go to Mr Ike's store, tell him to give me a bottle of palm oil, and I'll pay him in five weeks," she said. "But," he pointed out, "you took oil from Uncle Ike's neighbor's shop two days ago." She yelled at him and told him not to let Ike's neighbour see him with the palm oil he was supposed to collect from Ike's store. She later explained why she borrowed from so many people: some may forget what she had collected, while others may simply pardon - so she wouldn't have to pay back everything.

Mrs. Brown was washing dishes three years later when Mr. Ike's son, Chibuzo, came in and told her that he had lent N500 to her son, Kolade. But he needs the money now because the owner, the daughter of a military man, is nearby. While Chibuzo was speaking, Idara - the daughter of Madam Okon came along seeking her N300 borrowed by Kolade. Mrs. Brown called Kolade in rage, most likely because a military man was involved. She hadn't forgotten her boxing skills from her youth; in fact, she was known as Mike Tysoness back then. She knocked Kolade out with one blow. Kolade was hospitalised for two weeks as a result of that single punch. Mrs. Brown was forced to borrow money to cover the medical expenses.

what would the world be, if 80% of the world population are like you?

NOTE: The above story is simply a fiction, we regret any resemblance the characters may have with anybody.(funny?)

There is a lot to learn from this story. One of which is that children are quick to learn attitudes we unconsciously place before them. Parents, what would the world be, if 80% of the world population are like you? Mrs. Brown *taught* her son to be a borrower. Let us meditate on what the scripture says in Proverbs 22:7:

> *The rich rules over the poor, and the borrower is the slave of the lender.(RSV)*

Did you get that - the borrower is a SLAVE of the lender. Hence when you teach your kids to be debtors, you are preparing them to be slaves. What an unnoticed way to continue slave trade. While some countries are claiming that the era of slave trade is over, many are still involving in it. Let us say NO to SLAVE TRADE. Let us teach financial principles to our children.

EXERCISES

1. Is it proper for a child to grow into his teens without having an opportunity to make his bed and wash his plates or clothes?

2. Should children be given monetary allowance? Give reasons for your answer

3. From this chapter, what is referred to as *financial slave trade*?

CHAPTER SIX

SEX EDUCATION

This is another topic many parents would want to study and yet avoid talking about since they sometimes dread their kids asking them questions about sex. Others have already practised what they will say if such questions arise. It strikes a chord about a story I read; A little child came home from school with a form, entering the house and seeing his mother, he asked, "Mum, please what is SEX?'. The mother sat him down, happy that she had rehearsed this subject matter. "My son, 'My son', she said, and explained the anatomy of man, procreation and reproductive processes, how the sperm meets with the ova. After about twenty minutes of a sound lecture which was meticulously planned out, the son asked, 'Mum, how can I write it in one line, the form requires NAME... GRADE... SEX(M/F)?'.

As defined in "www.avert.org/sex-education.htm", 'Sex Education is the process of acquiring information and forming attitudes and beliefs about sex, sexual identity and relationships'. In sex education, a child is taught the skill of being able to identify pressures from other people and to resist them, and to be able to seek help from their parents.

Teenagers need proper sex education because the Bible says in Hosea 4:6 "my people are destroyed because of lack of knowledge". Lack of sex-related wisdom and knowledge could harm children. To prepare the kids for more advanced knowledge as they get older, we must first teach them the fundamentals appropriate for their age. As a parent, you should be able to train your child to recognise "inappropriate touching" from people'. The child should be able to resist it and later inform you about it. Hence, be close to your children. Despite the fact that it could be

People are destroyed because of lack of knowledge
Hosea 4:6

an uncomfortable process to talk with your children about sexuality, once you start, it becomes easier with time. "*Studies show that the more positive, value-centered sex education kids receive in their home, the less promiscuous they will be" - Jim Burns(2008).*

If your child asks you a question about sex, don't ignore him; it could be an opportunity to educate him.For we are living in a'sex-drive' information-driven society where even to advertise a shoe, you see an erotic scene in the media.

What some public schools teach as sex education is not a good value system but 'protected sex'. They sometimes encourage sexual comportment instead of giving age-appropriate information. It is a pity that what some people teach children and teenagers is "if you must have sex, use a condom. It is like saying to your child, "do not smoke, for it is dangerous to your health, but if you must smoke, use menthol to clear your mouth'. Condoms may prevent the transference of some diseases, but can they prevent the transference of spirits and the emotional problems associated with premarital sex? The Scripture says ... flee sexual immorality(1 Cor 6:18).

The teaching on sexual purity from the parent to the child is not a onetime lecture. It should be an "age-appropriate" discussion. Some parents argue that they were not taught sexuality by their own parents. Hence, they keep mute about it. Can we really afford to be quiet and let the media and other secular influences teach our children about sexuality? If you do not teach them, others will. John Chirban informs us that studies have confirmed that "kids today are learning more about sex from pornography than from their sex *education* classes. Middle-school children, let alone teens, are inundated with porn through the media and internet". Of course, the effect of pornography in our society today is not what you desire for the children that God blessed you with. Dear parents, you have every reason to guard your kids against the tricks of the devil.

It is also a fact that several teens find it difficult to express themselves or discuss sexuality with their parents. Hence, the parents could assist the teenager in finding a good mentor such as a teacher, counsellor or pastor (yet with caution).

> *Where no counsel is, the people fall: but in the multitude of counsellors there is safety.*
> ***Prov 11:14***

EXERCISES

1. Parents, if while going through your daughter's diary, you found out that she has been in a *dirty* relationship. At that point, she comes in seeing you studying her diary and she gets annoyed. What would you do?
   (a) Acknowledge the girl's feelings of hurt and make an effort to open lines of communication.
   (b) Become defensive/offensive and deal with her for being stupid.
(c) Disown her.

2. The teaching on sexual purity from the parent to the child is not a onetime lecture. TRUE or FALSE?

3. Are condoms the solution to the menace of sexual immorality? YES/NO

CHAPTER SEVEN

THE CAMERA

Garbage in Garbage out

Consider this illustration: you put on your best safari suit on the day of your convocation ceremony and went to the best photographic shops and posed for a photo shot. It was probably a wait-and-take picture. Two minutes after the shot, the picture rolled out, and behold, in the picture you saw your image in pyjamas, your hair - unkempt, looking like that of a monkey. What would be your reaction? Don't even mention it. The picture should not show something different from what was captured on the photographic film. It is like planting beans and seeing cassava germinating. It is like allowing our children to capture us with their photographic minds doing wrong, being lazy, living immoral lives, and expecting them to be good boys and girls.

'Action speaks louder than words' is a common adage. Be a mentor to your children. If your children became like you, what kind of world would we have? It should not be 'do what I say and not what I do'. There are drunkards today who get so annoyed seeing their children sipping alcohol and smoking. Some children are saying within themselves 'Dad cannot keep to what he says, why should I keep to it?' The Bible says concerning Jesus;

> ***Acts 1:1*** *The former treatise have I made, O Theophilus, of all that Jesus began both to <u>do</u> and <u>teach</u>*

The doing came before the teaching; Jesus began to <u>do</u> and to <u>teach</u>.

Parents - your children are watching you, they observe you and sometimes imitate you. You may even be oblivious of what your kids record in their minds. Let me relate to you a story from Dr H.J. Sala's book 'Train up a child and be glad you did' -

"*Little did one father realize that when he drove across town commenting on the ability of other drivers, he was also teaching his son. He finally learned what he was doing when someone asked, 'Billy, how was the trip?' The little boy replied, 'fine, but we saw three idiots, four fools, and two blankety-blanks on the road'. The father was embarrassed, naturally. He never expected his little boy to give a recital of what he had said ...*".

Spotted And Speckled

What kind of kids do you desire to have? Is it a child that would be a disgrace to you or a child that would bring joy to the home? Then you must watch your character. Dr. Marva Mitchell in her book titled "It takes a Church to raise a Village" mentioned that "One-third of the children who witness the battering of their mothers will go on to manifest significant behavioural problems. These deviant behaviours include psychosomatic disorders, stuttering anxiety, bed wetting, sleeping disorders. Coupled with displaying psychological symptoms, these kids will also *act out* their hurt and pain in school. This is exhibited in failing grades, skipping classes, fighting, and rebelling against school authorities"

> ***Genesis 30:37-39*** *Jacob cut branches from some poplar trees and from some almond and evergreen trees. He peeled off part of the bark and made the branches look spotted and speckled.*
>
> *Then he put the branches where the sheep and goats would* ***see*** *them while they were drinking from the water trough. The goats mated there in front of the branches, and their young were spotted and speckled. (CEV)*

What happened in Genesis 30:37 - 39 is a principle. The goats produced the image of the thing they saw. It is the principle of the camera, it produces what it sees. It works the same way with children, for what they constantly watch could be what they would replicate in their lifetime. Hence we should help our kids by censoring movies they watch. You would not consider it sane for a man to give his child a size 11 shoe when the child's feet is meant for size 5. Yet some parents see it as normal allowing their teen-child to watch films rated for adults. When they become 'spotted and speckled', it is only the product of what they were freely allowed to absorb. Take note: it is easier to train a child than to repair an adult. Let us look intently into the following scriptures:

Proverbs 23:7

For as he thinketh in his heart, so is he:... (KJV)

Matthew 15:11 Not that which goeth into the mouth defileth a man; but that which cometh out of the mouth, this defileth a man. (KJV)

Matthew 15:17-20 Do not ye yet understand, that whatsoever entereth in at the mouth goeth into the belly, and is cast out into the draught? But those things which proceed out of the mouth come forth from the heart; and they defile the man. For out of the heart proceed evil thoughts, murders, adulteries, fornications, thefts, false witness, blasphemies: These are the things which defile a man: but to eat with unwashen hands defileth not a man. (KJV)

Watch The Gates

There are several inputs into the human 'body'. There is the common phrase - Garbage in Garbage out - which is to say that what you get out of a computer system is a result of what was put into it. It is similar to the human being; several inputs exist such as the mouth, nose, eyes, ears etc.

The Mouth - input to the stomach (digestive system)

The Nose - input to the lungs (circulatory system)

The Eye and Ear - input to the MIND(Thinking System)

So when the scripture says 'as a man thinketh', it will be addressing the ear and the eye, not the mouth--thus Jesus said it is not what enters the mouth that defiles. The Bible says that out of the abundance of the heart, the mouth speaks(Matthew 12:34), hence Jesus said in verse 18 of Matthew 15, "Those things which proceed out of the mouth come from the heart(thinking system); and they defile the man'. Hence, let us, as parents, consciously censor what our kids (children, teenagers, and adolescents) watch and listen to. Josh McDowell rightly noted that "the inescapable fact is that both the media and our entire society are saturated with sex. The result is that our children are constantly bombarded with highly charged sexual messages encouraging promiscuity". Let us therefore be careful about what we allow our kids to watch. What they also listen to can affect them.

Sometimes children listen to their parents grumbling and complaining. Some parents complain about everything—the government, their boss, their spouse, and so on—while their children observe and learn. Do not make your children feel inferior, always encourage them wisely. There is this story of a man who went with his son to his school graduation and award ceremony. Many children were given awards, but none went to his son. When ever a child was called to collect his/her award, the man would look at his son and say, "These *are real children'.* The boy almost wept while his dad kept mocking him. At the end of the ceremony, they were going back home with their corroded and slow vehicle. Whenever a fine car or jeep overtook them, the son would look at the dad and say, "These *are real cars.* You know, kids are good imitators. You have the responsibility to teach them worthwhile things.

Teach your children the act of giving. Many children grow up always saying 'give me', they grow up stingy. The scripture says in **Acts 20:35,**"... *remember the words of the Lord Jesus, how he said, It is more blessed to give than to receive*". So teach them the more blessed path of giving. If you take the time to teach your children how to give, you will not be in need in your old age because your children will have mastered the act of giving and will always give to you. If you are a Christian and you go to church, give your children money to put in the offering bag. Sometimes, give them money to give to the poor and needy. Also inculcate in your children the need to trust and depend on God; that they may yearn for His presence always.

> **Psalms 118:8** It is better to trust in the LORD than to put confidence in man. (KJV)

The Prayer Of The Three Fishes

There is a story of three small fishes living in the sea. Small fishes were the normal day to day prey to the BIG fish. The three fishes decided to pray and the Creator asked them to make specific requests. Fish 'A' asked that it would have many eyes all around its body so that it could see afar to know when the Big fish is coming; 'GRANTED';

The fish, one day saw the Big fish coming from the north, hence it moved quickly towards the south and was able to jump out of the water on time into a little pool of water on the shore. soon after, the sun came up and the pool of water dried up, the fish could not go back to the sea. A child saw it, picked it up and straight to his mother's pot. Fish 'B' asked for wings like a dove so that when it senses danger it would fly out of the water; 'GRANTED'; The fish was so glad, it went to where the big fish was, and played around. The Big fish was surprised that the small fish was so confident, anyway it went for it, but the small fish mockingly said, "*even if you know me before o, you no go know me again*", and off, it flew out of the water singing the song of David in Psalm 55:6 ... Oh that I had wings like a dove! *for then* would I fly away, and be at rest.

So the fish kept flying; Then an Eagle saw it as a miracle, it had always wanted to eat fish, and miraculously a fresh fish was brought to its domain. The fish was eaten. Fish 'C' asked only for the presence of the Lord. When the Big fish came, it always saw a big shadow around the small fish so it went back and could not harm the fish.

Psalm 91:1 - 16

He that dwelleth in the secret place of the most High shall abide under the shadow of the Almighty.

I will say of the LORD, He is my refuge and my fortress: my God; in him will I trust. Surely he shall deliver thee from the snare of the fowler, and from the noisome pestilence. He shall cover thee with his feathers, and under his wings shalt thou trust: his truth shall be thy shield and buckler.

Thou shalt not be afraid for the terror by night; nor for the arrow that flieth by day; Nor for the pestilence that walketh in darkness; nor for the destruction that wasteth at noonday.

A thousand shall fall at thy side, and ten thousand at thy right hand; but it shall not come nigh thee. Only with thine eyes shalt thou behold and see the reward of the wicked.

Because thou hast made the LORD, which is my refuge, even the most High, thy habitation;

There shall no evil befall thee, neither shall any plague come nigh thy dwelling. For he shall give his angels charge over thee, to keep thee in all thy ways. They shall bear thee up in their hands, lest thou dash thy foot against a stone.

Thou shalt tread upon the lion and adder: the young lion and the dragon shalt thou trample under feet. Because he hath set his love upon me, therefore will I deliver him: I will set him on high, because he hath known my name.

He shall call upon me, and I will answer him: I will be with him in trouble; I will deliver him, and honour him. With long life will I satisfy him, and shew him my salvation. (KJV)

What then can I say, 'if God be for us, who can be against us'. Your children need to know this GOD.

EXERCISES

1. Is it necessary to censor films watched by our children?

2. The Eye and Ear are inputs to __________

(a) Digestive system
(b) Thinking system
(c) Circulatory system

3. Which is not part of the things parents should teach their kids?

(a) Giving
(b) Complaining
(c) Seeking God

4. Mention some behavioural attributes you desire in your kids. How many of such attributes do you have?

CHAPTER EIGHT

ADVICE TO PARENTS

(1) Love and Respect your spouse:

Let us consider the following scripture.

> ***Colossians 3:18-20***
>
> *Wives, submit yourselves unto your own husbands, as it is fit in the Lord.*
>
> *Husbands, love your wives, and be not bitter against them.*
>
> *Children, obey your parents in all things: for this is well pleasing unto the Lord.*

Many parents stress verse 20 of the above passage without considering the sequence of 18-19-20. When the wife submits to her OWN husband, it becomes easy for verse 19 to take shape. And when the wife submits and the husband shows her true love, it becomes easy for verse 20 to take shape. Have you not noticed that when there is strife in a home, and the parents are always fighting - the kids tend to be wild. It is clearly written in the Bible;

James 3:16 For where envying and strife is, there is confusion and every evil work.(KJV)

Can you imagine where every kind of evil work such as kidnapping, rape, robbery, lesbianism, homosexuality and the likes comes from? Should we sell our children to these evils because we do not want to love, respect and submit to our spouse?

Let me reiterate with the Message Version of the Bible

> ***Colossians 3:18-19***
>
> *Wives, understand and support your husbands by submitting to them in ways that honour the Master.*
>
> *Husbands, go all out in love for your wives. Don't take advantage of them.*

(Message Version)

As a wife, do you truly make effort to understand your husband to be able to whole-heartedly support his visions? (Someone may be asking, "*does he even have a vision*?")

As a husband, have you gone all out in love for your OWN wife. Please do not take advantage of her submissiveness. If we all can follow God's outline for marriage - our society would be better for it.

(2) Concentrate on your child's good points, and don't overemphasize his failings.

Sometimes kids want to be considered as 'heroes'. They want to be famous, not bothering themselves with what makes them known. If he steals, discipline him and correct him. If you as a parent overemphasize it, shouting through the streets and calling him names like 'Big Thief' or 'Correct Thief', and his friends nick name him 'Thief-o-o' or 'Big T'. That could make him famous, and he will do more to continue with his title as 'Big T'. If, on the other hand, you emphasize his good deeds, he will desire to improve. While in junior secondary school, I struggled with mathematics; however, in senior secondary, I resolved to give it my all in order to excel at it. Praise God, it worked. I had the highest score in the maths test, and the teacher wrote on my test script, "See me *in the staff room"*. There he told my physics teacher that I was a very bright student (he advertised me) - I told myself that I must do well in physics to prove the maths teacher right. So it was, then they advertised me to the Chemistry teacher , "don't you know this boy, he is very brilliant'. Hmm, I had to start doing well in that subject too. *I wish they also advertised me to the English teacher...*

Praise 'effort' rather than 'success'; your child/ward may have put in great efforts, for instance, studying very hard for an exam but did not get an 'A', do not crucify him, encourage him! We often look for opportunities to catch our teenagers doing wrong so that we can discipline them severely; however, I encourage you to begin looking for more opportunities to catch them doing right so that you can praise them. Be a 'good-finder' rather than a 'fault-finder'.

(3) Make clear rules, enforce them with consistent discipline:

Children can easily predict when you are not serious. Consider a father telling his child, 'don't do that or else I will flog you'. The child repeats it and he says, "Can't you hear me? I'll flog you'. The child repeats it and he says, "When I beat you now, you'll start crying—till I flog you, you'll know' (clear rules but no enforcement). Other times, you may have clear rules which you enforce but not consistently. So the child grows up with the knowledge that you will repeat yourself up to ten times before you take action. Parents should not give divergent and contradictory rules. The father says, 'do not go there' while the mother says, 'You may go but do not stay there for a long period'. I subscribe to Dr. H.J. Sala's suggestion—"if your mate makes a decision and you disagree, support him in the decision and then talk it out privately—out of the hearing of the children. To come up with split opinion not only hurts your child, but your relationship with your mate".

(4) Make your children to know why they are being punished :

Some parents do not bother informing their child of the offence he has committed. Consider that you told your teenage child/ward not to tell a lie but that whenever he makes a mistake, he should endeavour to apologize. Days later, the child breaks a glass cup and says he was not the one who broke it until you were able to find out the truth. If you discipline that child, probably by the use of the cane, you should be able to make it clear whether you flogged him for telling a lie or for breaking the glass cup(which could be unintentional).

That 'houseboy' of yours probably saw you coughing and, in a bid to help, ran to get a glass of water for you. And while running, he slipped and the glass broke. What would you do? Some folks love property more than life. They would not ask if the child was injured. All their concern is, "I hope it is not the sound of the glass cup that I am hearing." A man saw through his window, his little curious child writing using his finger through the dust on his daddy's new car. The dad ran out in anger, took the child, kicked him, slapped him till he fainted. 'Why must he go near the new car? Does he know how much it costs?" yelled the Dad while he left the child on the floor in pain, and went to check the car. He saw what the little child was writing - My daddy is the best daddy, I love my daddy!!! The man fell down, regretting his actions.

(5) Do not cause them to enter their shell:

A snail has a protective shell and when it feels insecure; it goes into it and would not respond. We should seek to be close to our teenagers, let them be free to discuss with us. If you let them go into their shell, things may go wrong and you may know of it only when it's too late.

> ***Ephesians 6:4*** *And, ye fathers, provoke not your children to wrath: but bring them up in the nurture and admonition of the Lord. (KJV)*

Colossians 4:6 *Let your speech be alway with grace, seasoned with salt, that ye may know how ye ought to answer every man. (KJV)*

Colossians 4:6 *Be gracious in your speech. The goal is to bring out the best in others in a conversation, not put them down, not cut them out. (Message Bible)*

Colossians 3:21 *Parents, don't come down too hard on your children or you'll crush their spirits. (The Message Bible)*

Proverbs 16:24 - 25 *Pleasant words are as an honeycomb, sweet to the soul, and health to the bones. There is a way that seemeth right unto a man, but the end thereof are the ways of death. (KJV)*

It takes grace and discipline to speak pleasant words when angry but it is worth it. One major cause of children entering their shell is the unguarded use of words by their parents. You may be familiar with words such as;

- "Is it the little thing I said that is making you sad? Go and die"
- "What you just said is the most stupid thing I have ever heard"
- "You are too dull. You need to grow up"

Colossians 4:6 in the Message version says you should not put them down nor cut them out.

There are signs which may indicate when your teenager is entering his or her shell.

- When the teenager begins to show lack of respect for your advice
- When the teenager avoids discussing with you
- When the teenager consciously disobeys you, such as going to places you warned against.
- When the teenager develops an argumentative attitude.

(6) If you have disciplined him - FORGIVE:

Your child committed an error, and is disciplined, why not forgive him. Do not continue to dwell on his mistakes. Some parents probably have a diary where they record each wrong their children commit till *their cup gets full.*

> ***Matthew 18:21 - 22*** *Then came Peter to him, and said, Lord, how oft shall my brother sin against me, and I forgive him? till seven times?*

Jesus saith unto him, I say not unto thee, Until seven times: but, Until seventy times seven. (KJV)

Peter acted as many parents would do today - having a diary of records. He hoped that seven wrongs would get the cup full but Jesus said to him, 'seventy times seven'. That is four hundred and ninety times. You may need to get a bigger diary - funny?

> ***Luke 11:4*** *Forgive our sins, as we forgive everyone who has done wrong to us. And keep us from being tempted.' "*

EXERCISES

1. What are the effects of over-emphasizing your child's failure?

2. Mention some signs that indicate a child entering his shell.

3. What steps can you take to be a *'good-finder'* instead of a *'fault-finder'*, and what can you do to encourage your child to continue doing good?

If you have not dedicated yourself to serve the Lord your maker, have a rethink. God gave you the power of choice. Please choose to serve Him. For you to read this far, you have a desire to bring forth responsible and God-fearing children. In training them properly - you cannot give what you do not have. Why not be responsible first and it would be easier to bring up responsible kids. As you come to the Lord, Be blessed in Jesus Name. Amen.

You can write to me

Nwankwo, Abinye D. C.
CHILDREN MINISTRY
Chapel of the Transfiguration
Ignatius Ajuru University of Education
Rumuolumeni, PMB 5047
Port Harcourt.

Or Email
abinyenwankwo@yahoo.com
+2348033805280

FEEDBACK PAGE

We would like to know the area in which this book has been a blessing to you.

We would like to hear your experience in training and disciplining of your children and wards

We would like to hear your questions about the subject matter.

Send us your questions, testimonies, experiences and even criticisms. It could help someone in future editions.

All correspondence to;
Commandingwealth.ng@gmail.com or
abinyenwankwo@yahoo.com or
Nwankwo, Abinye D. C.
CHILDREN MINISTRY
Chapel of the Transfiguration
Ignatius Ajuru University of Education
Rumuolumeni, PMB 5047. Port Harcourt.

REFERENCES

Dr. Marva Mitchell, It Takes a Church to raise a Village, Destiny Image Publishers, Inc, USA, 2001

Gary Smalley & Greg Smalley, the DNA of Parent-Teen Relationships, Mindex Publishing Co. Ltd, Nigeria, 2005

Harold J. Sala, Train Up A Child-And be glad you did, Accent-B/P Publications, 1978.

John T. Chirban, In the Age of Un-Innocence, www.psychologytoday.com/blog/the-age-un-innocence/201212/pornographythe-new-sex-ed-kids (15 Dec 2012)

Nancy Lloyd, Children: The ABCs of Allowances - http://www.ivillage.com/childrenthe-abcs-allowances/6-a-128687 (1 Jan 1999)

Microsoft® Encarta® 2009. © 1993-2008 Microsoft Corporation

ABOUT THE AUTHOR

Abinye Nwankwo is a multitalented person. A combination of great qualities from his late parents, Rev. Canon Israel A. Nwankwo and Dr. Mrs. Joyce N. Nwankwo has greatly influenced his lifestyle. He is hard-working and meticulous. He is a creative entrepreneur who has mentored several people in the development of their skills.

Engr Abinye Nwankwo earned a bachelor's degree in Electrical/Electronics Engineering before pursuing a master's degree in Electronics/Telecommunications. He also possessed a master's degree in Engineering

Management. He is a member of Nigeria's Council for the Regulation of Engineering (COREN)

Uncle Abinye, as he is commonly known, has been inspiring talented children and teenagers for over twenty years. He is a gifted and inspirational writer who has written several influential books, including "Creating your season of Abundance," "The hurdle (fiction)," "Thy Kingdom come," "Strange things in Zion," "Emphasizing Dominion - as God intended," "The Ecclesiastical Epistles," and others.

He is enthusiastic about teaching God's word. And he is always willing to learn more.

He is happily married to Dr. Mrs. Mercy Nwankwo, with whom he has five biological children (the E-series). Many other children look up to him and his wife as parents.

www.ingramcontent.com/pod-product-compliance
Lightning Source LLC
LaVergne TN
LVHW050319160826
845677LV00014B/3482

* 9 7 9 8 3 5 4 1 9 3 2 3 3 *